SUPER SIMPLE
Pinecone Projects

FUN AND EASY CRAFTS INSPIRED BY NATURE

Kelly Doudna

Consulting Editor, Diane Craig, M.A./Reading Specialist

A Division of ABDO

ABDO
Publishing Company

visit us at www.abdopublishing.com

Published by ABDO Publishing Company, a division of ABDO, P.O. Box 398166, Minneapolis, Minnesota 55439.
Copyright © 2014 by Abdo Consulting Group, Inc. International copyrights reserved in all countries. No part of this book may be reproduced in any form without written permission from the publisher. Super SandCastle™ is a trademark and logo of ABDO Publishing Company.

Printed in the United States of America, North Mankato, Minnesota
102013
012014

PRINTED ON RECYCLED PAPER

Editor: Liz Salzmann
Content Developer: Nancy Tuminelly
Cover and Interior Design and Production: Kelly Doudna, Mighty Media, Inc.
Photo Credits: Kelly Doudna, Shutterstock

The following manufacturers/names appearing in this book are trademarks: Aleene's® Tacky Glue®, Elmer's®

Library of Congress Cataloging-in-Publication Data
Doudna, Kelly, 1963-
  Super simple pinecone projects : fun and easy crafts inspired by nature / Kelly Doudna, consulting editor,
Diane Craig, M.A./reading specialist.
     pages cm. -- (Super simple nature crafts)
  Audience: Age 5-10.
  ISBN 978-1-62403-080-2
1. Pine cone craft--Juvenile literature. 2. Nature craft--Juvenile literature. I. Title.
  TT874.5.D68 2014
  745.594--dc23
                           2013022899

Super SandCastle™ books are created by a team of professional educators, reading specialists, and content developers around five essential components—phonemic awareness, phonics, vocabulary, text comprehension, and fluency—to assist young readers as they develop reading skills and strategies and increase their general knowledge. All books are written, reviewed, and leveled for guided reading, early reading intervention, and Accelerated Reader® programs for use in shared, guided, and independent reading and writing activities to support a balanced approach to literacy instruction.

to adult Helpers

The craft projects in this series are fun and simple. There are just a few things to remember to keep kids safe. Some projects require the use of sharp or hot objects. Also, kids may be using messy materials such as glue or paint. Make sure they protect their clothes and work surfaces. Review the projects before starting, and be ready to assist when necessary.

key symbols

In this book, you will see some warning symbols. Here is what they mean.

HOT!
You will be working with something hot. Get help!

SHARP!
You will be working with a sharp object. Get help!

contents

Pretty Pinecones

We love the smell of pine needles. We love to kick pinecones around in the backyard. Take a nature walk. See how many different kinds of pinecones you can find.

Then it's time to go inside and get creative! Try the fun and simple projects in this book. You'll be pleased with the pinecone perfection you produce!

aBOut Pinecones

Pinecones are the way **conifer** trees make and scatter seeds. Cones can be short and round. They can be long and narrow.

The Canadian hemlock tree makes the smallest cones. They are only 1 inch (2.5 cm). The sugar pine tree makes the longest cones. They can be 24 inches (61 cm) long. And don't stand under a Coulter pine tree. Its cone can weigh up to 10 pounds (4.5 kg). You don't want that to hit your head!

Coulter pine pinecone

sugar pine pinecone

Canadian hemlock branch and pinecones

PINECONES IN THIS BOOK

We used small, **medium**, and large pinecones for the projects in this book.

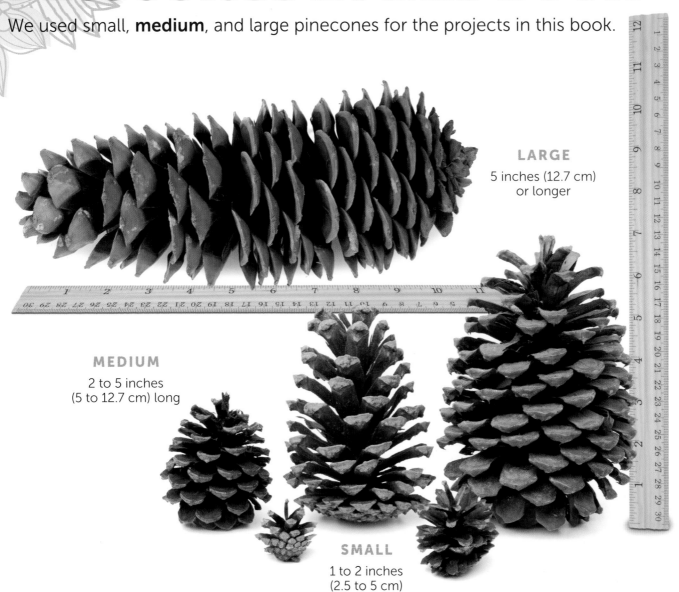

LARGE
5 inches (12.7 cm)
or longer

MEDIUM
2 to 5 inches
(5 to 12.7 cm) long

SMALL
1 to 2 inches
(2.5 to 5 cm)

Preparing Pinecones

It's a good idea to bake your pinecones before you use them. Baking kills any bugs that may have come along for the ride!

1 Heat the oven to 250 **degrees**.

2 Put aluminum foil on the baking sheet. Lay your pinecones on the foil.

3 Bake for 45 minutes. Remove the baking sheet from the oven. Let the pinecones cool.

MATERIALS

baking sheet
aluminum foil
pinecones
oven mitts

PRO TIP

Pinecones open up when they dry out. If you want a closed pinecone, soak it in cold water right after you take it out of the oven.

FUN FACT

The "leaves" of a pinecone are called scales. They are also called petals or wings.

WHat you'll need

Here are many of the things you will need to do the projects in this book. You can find some of them around the house or yard. You can get others at a craft store or hardware store.

pinecones

paper plates

glue

glitter

ribbon

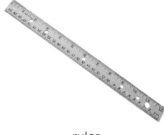

ruler

hot glue gun
and glue sticks

cotton balls

craft glue

pom-poms

googly eyes

chenille stems

wooden beads

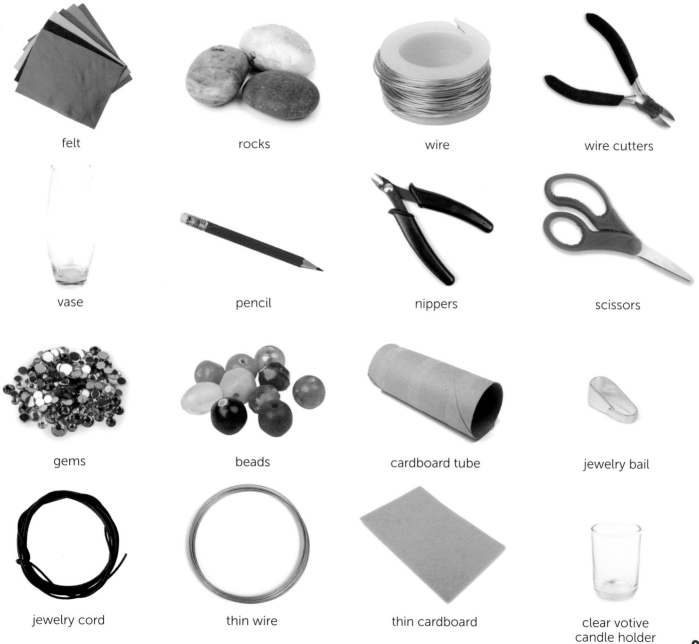

felt

rocks

wire

wire cutters

vase

pencil

nippers

scissors

gems

beads

cardboard tube

jewelry bail

jewelry cord

thin wire

thin cardboard

clear votive
candle holder

9

glittery pinecones

Spread some sparkle with pinecones that glimmer and shimmer.

WHAT YOU'LL NEED

pinecones
all-purpose glue
paper plate
glitter
spray fixative
(optional)

10

1 Put a drop of glue on each pinecone scale.

2 Hold the pinecone over a paper plate. Sprinkle glitter over the pinecone.

3 Gently shake off the extra glitter. Let the glue dry.

4 You may want to spray the pinecone with fixative. This helps hold the glitter in place.

 get fancy

Glue some glitter to the underside of each scale too. It will **sparkle** from every angle!

 fun fact

Both pine trees and fir trees have cones. A pine tree's needles are grouped in bunches. A fir tree's needles are single.

ornaments

Catch the light with these glittery decorations.

1 Make a Glittery Pinecone. (see pages 10 and 11). Use glitter that matches the ribbon.

2 Cut a 10-inch (25.4 cm) piece of ribbon.

3 Tie the ribbon to the top of the pinecone.

4 Tie the ends of the ribbon together.

get fancy
Use sparkly ribbon to give your ornament extra shine!

winter scene

Make a sparkly winter wonderland.

WHAT YOU'LL NEED

pinecones

all-purpose glue

paper plate

glitter

spray fixative (optional)

hot glue gun and glue sticks

cotton balls

1 Make a few Glittery Pinecones (see pages 10 and 11).

2 Arrange the Glittery Pinecones on a paper plate. Glue them to the plate with hot glue.

3 Pull apart some cotton balls.

4 Put all-purpose glue on the paper plate. Cover the plate with cotton. Fit it around the pinecones.

get fancy

Add a snowman to your scene! Glue three cotton balls together. Glue on small gems for the eyes and buttons. Glue on a piece of string for the smile.

forest friends

You'll have an animal adventure when you create these cute critters.

WHAT YOU'LL NEED

regular and fuzzy chenille stems

ruler

scissors

medium pinecones

craft glue

pom-poms in different sizes and colors

googly eyes

wooden bead

felt

Squirrel

1 **TAIL.** Cut an 8-inch (20.3 cm) piece of fuzzy chenille stem. Fold it in half. Twist the ends together. Glue the twisted end to the bottom of the pinecone. Bend it up to make the squirrel's tail.

2 **HEAD.** Glue two googly eyes to a large pom-pom. Cut two 1-inch (2.5 cm) pieces of chenille stem. Fold each into a "v" to make the ears. Glue the ends to the top of the head. Glue on a small piece of chenille stem for the mouth. Glue the head to the top of the pinecone.

3 **ACORN.** Cut a 1-inch (2.5 cm) piece of chenille stem. Wind it into the shape of an acorn cap and stem. Glue it to the side of the wooden bead. Don't glue it over the hole.

4 **ARMS.** Cut a 5-inch (12.7 cm) piece of regular chenille stem. Thread it through the acorn. Glue the ends to the sides of the pinecone.

Rabbit

1 **HEAD.** Glue two googly eyes to a large pom-pom. Glue a tiny pom-pom right below the eyes. Glue two more tiny pom-poms below the first one. These three pom-poms make the rabbit's **muzzle**.

2 **EARS.** Cut two pieces of felt in the shape of rabbit ears. Make them about 3 inches (7.6 cm) long. **Crease** the ears the long way. Glue them to the back of the head. Glue the head to the top of the pinecone.

3 **TAIL.** Glue a white pom-pom to the back of the pinecone.

Owl

1 FACE. Cut two felt circles a little larger than the googly eyes. Glue a googly eye to each circle. Glue the eyes to the top of the pinecone. Cut a 1-inch (2.5 cm) piece of yellow chenille stem. Fold it into a "v" to make the beak. Glue the ends to the pinecone under the eyes.

2 FEET. Cut two 4-inch (10.2 cm) pieces of chenille stem. Bend three points into each piece. Spread the points apart to make toes. Twist the ends together. Glue both feet to the bottom of the pinecone. The toes should point forward.

3 WINGS. Use two colors of felt. Cut two wing shapes out of one color. Cut two smaller wing shapes out of the other color. Glue each small piece onto a large piece. Glue a wing to each side of the pinecone.

BOBBLEHEADS

The ballpark isn't the only place to bobble.

20

WHAT YOU'LL NEED

rocks
pinecones
thin wire
ruler
wire cutters
pencil

1. Gather a few rocks. They should fit in the palm of your hand. Gather the same number of pinecones.

2. Cut a 24-inch (61 cm) piece of wire. Wrap one end around a rock. Twist it closed at the top of the rock. The long end of the wire should be sticking up.

3. Wrap the wire around the pencil. Start close to the rock. Leave 6 inches (15.2 cm) at the end of the wire straight. Pull the pencil out of the **coil**.

4. Wrap the end of the wire around the bottom of a pinecone. Twist it closed. Bend the wire so the pinecone sticks up from the rock.

5. Repeat steps 2 through 4 with the rest of the rocks and pinecones.

🐦 fun tip

Put a group of bobbleheads in the middle of the dinner table. They'll make an entertaining **centerpiece**!

flowers

Use these pretty flowers in plenty of places.

WHAT YOU'LL NEED

pinecones

nippers

ruler

felt

scissors

hot glue gun and glue sticks

gems or beads

wire

wire cutters

vase

cardboard tubes

wide ribbon

craft glue

jewelry bail

jewelry cord

22

Pinecone Flower

1 Use the nippers to cut some scales off a pinecone. Cut a 1-inch (2.5 cm) felt circle.

2 Hot glue the largest scales around the outside of the felt. The cut ends should face the center.

3 Glue another circle of scales inside the first one.

4 Glue a gem or bead in the center of the flower.

Pinecone Flower Bouquet

Make several Pinecone Flowers. Hot glue a 12-inch (30.5 cm) piece of wire to the back of each flower. Arrange the flowers in a vase.

Napkin Rings

1 Cut a piece of paper towel tube that's the same width as the ribbon. Cut a piece of ribbon long enough to wrap around the tube.

2 Put craft glue on the back of the ribbon. Wrap the ribbon around the tube.

3 Put a drop of hot glue on the **seam** of the ribbon. Press a Pinecone Flower (see page 23) into the glue. Let the glue dry.

4 Repeat steps 1 through 3 to make more **napkin** rings.

 PRO TIP

Putting the flower on the seam hides the seam. This makes the napkin ring look better!

Pinecone Pendant

1 Hot glue a bail to the back of a Pinecone Flower (see page 23).

2 Cut a piece of cord long enough to slip over your head plus 4 inches (10.2 cm). Thread the cord through the bail.

3 Tie the ends of the cord together. Cut off the ends of the cord close to the knot.

 variation

Make a giant pendant! Cut a 3-inch (7.6 cm) felt circle for step 1 of the Pinecone Flower (see page 23). Make four or five circles of scales on the felt. Make sure they cover the felt circle. Glue a gem or bead in the center. Then follow the Pinecone Pendant steps above.

PHOTO HOLDER

Unique photo holders will help you hang on to your memories.

WHAT YOU'LL NEED

thin wire

ruler

wire cutters

beads

hot glue gun and glue sticks

pinecone

1 Cut an 8-inch (20.3 cm) piece of wire. Wind it into a circle with one and a half loops. Leave at least 1 inch (2.5 cm) straight.

2 Thread the beads onto the wire until they are at the bottom of the loop.

3 Put a drop of hot glue on the top of the pinecone. Poke the straight end of the wire into the glue. Hold the wire in place while the glue sets. Let the glue dry.

4 Slip a **photo** between the loops.

get fancy
Use a Glittery Pinecone (see pages 10 and 11) for your photo holder.

CANDLE HOLDER

Get a good glow going with these cute cups.

WHAT YOU'LL NEED

clear votive candle holder

thin cardboard

pencil

ruler

scissors

pinecones

nippers

hot glue gun and glue sticks

sparkly chenille stem

1 Set the candle holder on the cardboard. Trace around it. Add ½ inch (1.3 cm) around the outside of the circle. Cut around the larger circle.

2 Use the nippers to cut some scales off of pinecones. How many you need depends on the size of the pinecones.

3 Glue the cut ends of the scales to the cardboard. Place them between the edge and the circle you traced.

continued on the next page

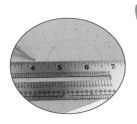

 PRO tiP
Use a ruler to measure the extra ½ inch around the traced circle. Make tick marks all the way around to guide your cutting.

29

4 Make another circle of scales. Glue them over the spaces between the scales in the first circle.

5 Continue gluing scales in circles. Stop when the sides are about as tall as the candle holder.

6 Wrap a sparkly chenille stem around the base of the pinecone holder. This will hide the edge of the cardboard circle. Use a drop of hot glue to hold it in place.

 Pro tip

The cardboard circle should be large enough to make a good base for the scales. But it should not be so large that you can see the cardboard under the scales. If the scales are small, make the circle a little smaller. If they are big scales, make the circle a little bigger.

 Get fancy

Hot glue some pine **sprigs** around the base of the pinecone candle holder.

conclusion

Aren't pinecones great? You have let the beauty of nature come through with these wonderful pinecone crafts. If you had fun, don't stop here. How else can you use pinecones?

And check out the other books in the Super Simple Nature Crafts series. You'll find projects that use ice, leaves, pressed flowers, seashells, and twigs. The ideas are endless!

glossary

centerpiece – a decoration, such as flowers or candles, in the center of a table.

coil – a spiral or a series of loops.

conifer – a tree that has needles instead of leaves and has cones for its seeds.

crease – to make a sharp line in something by folding it.

degree – the unit used to measure temperature.

medium – not the largest or the smallest.

muzzle – the nose and jaws of an animal.

napkin – a square piece of paper or cloth used to protect the clothes while eating and to wipe hands and lips.

photo – a picture made using a camera.

seam – the line where two edges meet.

sparkle – to shine with flashes of light.

sprig – a small twig or shoot of a tree or plant.